Praise for ALL THE BLOOD INVO

"Confounded, mesmerized, and enraged, women gaze rejoice and recoil at the possibility of sons and the sudd of sons. Craving just one unconquered root, they collect and shed lovers, some who are quivering mirrors, some edges that might be blades. Fathers boom tenet from every crevice. Never quite pinpointing the source of pain, women clutch tight their own bodies to hold in the hurricane. This work—penned as backslap for the Black woman intending to stomp into, through, and beyond the existence she is laughingly 'allowed'—harbors the hurricane's unrepentant muscle. Enter and risk. Enter and live." —PATRICIA SMITH, author of *Incendiary Art*

"*All the Blood Involved in Love* is at once the most southern, most feminist, and Blackest book I have ever read. Maya Marshall witnesses the way we used that word in the old church, through a language so polished and exact that we feel cleansed by it as readers. This is a beautiful debut from a game-changing poet." —JERICHO BROWN, author of *The Tradition*

"*All the Blood Involved in Love* is a lyrical work of psychological and temporal complexity gripped by questions of freedom, trauma, desire, imagination, and possibilities of Black girlhood and womanhood in the US. It is at once sensuous and terrifying, taut and lush, as in: 'Do these trees know? / Do these trees know the grazing hem, the line / between sweet heat and deep sweat? // The woman('s) sex. Her hanging. They must. / Her hair is made of them.' I'm saying, this stunningly shiftful, strange, and exact book interrogates the histories with which our blood and time are written. It insists that there is power in such scrutiny. I'm saying, her Eye's on this: 'To save my life, I undress this disarray.'" —ARACELIS GIRMAY, author of *the black maria*

"Maya Marshall's *All the Blood Involved in Love* sounds the breadth and depth of embodied Black womanhood. This poet holds her pen to the fire and writes in flame, lines that are passionate yet brutally precise. Black women move through the poems in relation to various families—biological, chosen, longed for, remembered, imagined, or barely escaped. Hear me: Marshall's poetry collects and confronts some of our knottiest questions, our hardest truths. But it also illuminates the connections that buoy and strengthen us, the knowing that enables us to thrive." —EVIE SHOCKLEY, author of *semiautomatic*

"Intimate and understated in unflinching private, public mourning, *All the Blood Involved in Love* courses with an undeniable, steady intensity throbbing at its tender jugular. Delivered with unnerving focus—almost unbearable—and declarative observations, we don't just read Maya Marshall's poems, we breathe with them and bleed with them: 'Tenderness is the impulse to protect / what you know you could destroy. / This is the gift of my father's neck.' This is a harrowing and illuminating book, surging with intelligence and pulsing with new music. Maya Marshall writes with life-force." —ROBYN SCHIFF, author of *Revolver*

All the Blood Involved in Love

MAYA MARSHALL

Haymarket Books
Chicago, Illinois

Published in 2022 by
Haymarket Books
P.O. Box 180165
Chicago, IL 60618
773-583-7884
www.haymarketbooks.org
info@haymarketbooks.org

ISBN: 978-1-64259-695-3

Distributed to the trade in the US through Consortium Book Sales and Distribution (www.cbsd.com) and internationally through Ingram Publisher Services International (www.ingramcontent.com).

This book was published with the generous support of Lannan Foundation and Wallace Action Fund.

Special discounts are available for bulk purchases by organizations and institutions. Please email info@haymarketbooks.org for more information.

Cover artwork, *The Black Unicorn,* by Rachel Eliza Griffiths.
Cover design by Rachel Cohen.

Printed in Canada by union labor.

Library of Congress Cataloging-in-Publication data is available.

10 9 8 7 6 5 4 3 2 1

To mothers, especially mine.

And to those who choose not to.

Memory is a mosquito, pregnant again, and out for blood.

—Gayl Jones,
from "Wild Figs and Secret Places"

God only had sons, according to Christians.
That tells you some of the trouble with God.

—Terrance Hayes,
from *To Float in the Space Between*

CONTENTS

I

II

I

"Why Don't You Parent a Little?"

The story is that there is so much loss,

so much waste in a woman who does not make

a body with her body. Such sunk potential

in a sex that does not produce.

The story is that we have progressed.

The story is that the black woman is safe.

The story is that the black woman is safe

if she protects her king.

The king is dead.

Long Live the Queen

in a corner of a covered
porch outside a house
that never belonged to us

hung a dung-gum
dangling palace
dual bodies hummed

inside my parents' marriage
a dry corn cob
the whole husk rattlehiss

in the spring hornets buzzed
never slick with anything
sweet like honey

Some Thoughts on Sons
in the Winter of My Child-Bearing Years

Where I'm from,

a mother births a son, finds it hard to love an absence.

*

I have never been a black boy, but I have always loved castaways.

*

I ask K— why he doesn't walk on lit major streets.
He says he is afraid to be outside in his body.

*

In a museum, a white woman reaches for me

tells me she's never thought
of black men being afraid.

*

When I say "son" I mean the corona blistering,
bright, covered in shadows, a circumference of dark flames
wavering.

*

In an alternate life, I adopt. My son calls me by my first name
until his first mother is only sense memory. He calls me mother and thief.

*

A smoker, single with a near teenager, a cat asleep on the couch.
My boy's neck and forehead. His shoulder blades bent toward his spine
like wings.
Late to gray, proud in my office, I scribble at my desk.

*

In the family I remember
one son takes, only ever takes,
rarely says sentences
that don't begin and end with lack
and a daughter's name.

*

In the origin story, a little boy, four feet tall,
puts his hand in a woman's brown hand.
He is led to a Volvo, asked about his day.
He raises his brown eyes to the woman's brown face,
examines the eyebrows, the lines on her forehead, before he says
"We learned about exoplanets, exoskeletons."

There is a light rain on his knees.

*

By *childhood* I mean bathtubs and closets, open doors
to moving cars and big brothers cycling in and out between moving
boxes and rain on sunny days.
We call that the devil beating his wife.

*

When I remember the man that I wanted to marry but couldn't,
I think about the children we didn't have.

My fibroids would have made room.
My love and I would have returned to sex with blood mixed in.

*

Bless the diva cup, bless the bloody penis. Bless
the boy I haven't conceived.

Daddy on the Sofa

The soft satellite of my father's ear falls
toward his shoulder. His chin floats up
from his clavicle. While the giant sleeps,
I wash the sharps in the kitchen sink.
When some breathing thing is vulnerable,
I understand the impulse to crush.
I'm inclined to pierce its softness.
Tenderness is the impulse to protect
what you know you could destroy.
This is the gift of my father's neck.

Baptism

Last night my brother called. We made promises.
Don't leave me alone with our mother while she's dying.

Promise me you won't be her or her mother: blue light
single women, amber oil on bulbs, sleeping in ashes

and urine with nine dogs to replace her living children.
I do. I remember when I would pray. I would talk to the belly

I came from, murmur to it, rest my cheek
on its sag and C-shaped scar. I remember us singing each other

to sleep. I can dream what not to be: blue notes, "Don't Smoke in Bed,"
anti-anxiety meds, baskets of paper, piles of clothes, death by rebirth.

I still remember who she was: energy crystals, books:
books for interpreting dreams. The Bible. Books for interpreting

numbers. The Bible. Tarot cards. The Bible. Marquees. She was light
and dazzle—her name in jumbo letters. Her sinner-self died in water,

left a stranger behind. All her stories, loves, lovers,
drowned in baptism. She rose, still broken, to live in wait, to die eventually.

The truth is, we—her children—won't find her.
Instead, we guess which will win: the depression or the diabetes?

Imagine we find her in melted ice cream. The truth: we don't
find her. She sleeps, cigarette in hand, burns the house down.

Charred puppy bones. Or she falls. The truth: we, her children,
don't talk the right way. There's too much poison in guilt.

Her assistant finds her. Or the friend who prays
with her. He's the last man to touch her hands in love.

I don't remember the last time we prayed together,
but my heart wants to be faithful. I love to touch her hands,

the yellow curve where she holds her cigarettes. I remember her stories.
I'll build a house of old stories, no-longer loves, tales for my nieces.

She can live with me when it's time to wash
her softest parts, hear her final secrets, watch her next rebirth.

Eviction

Her sisters carry her things to the stoop.
Six dachshunds herd the fur she hasn't cleaned,
chase hard diabetic feet up, down the
winding wrought iron staircase. Tomorrow

she will miss all of her rooms. True, no room
or man was ever hers at all. She has
been waiting for God to pay. She has been
winding yarn in the absence of filters, ash.

Each year leaving home brings her closer
to its every chamber—each block and sibling.
She has been waiting for all of these years.
Untethered, she will not look to her mother,

the wrinkles of her, the sag she made when
she filled her, the stretch marks that surround the
exit wound, nor wonder that we return
by necessity. We return by necessity.

Musing on Lilith Lost to Time

The myth is Grandaddy's mother
birthed twelve children
by twelve discrete men. I asked what she did for work
and my big brother (of a different father)
laughed at my insinuation
that sex could be her job.
As if being a whore is a joke, a lark. As if she
a ground-dwelling songbird
with her streaky brown plumage,
didn't shift her bones to shape the world
twelve times. It was America, after all.
It was 1930 to 1953. It was Beaufort,
South Carolina, and a woman
is her own business. What's so funny?
How many times did she make the shape of the sky
with her legs, the oblong sphere of the earth
with her belly? How many times was she an ossuary?
Lilith with her crooked feet
maybe could only deliver her song
in flight, crest pressed forward by her back's arc,
belly swollen from fucking in that good
sweet way women do when they want to.

Lavender Menace Considers Adoption

I'm so American I close my ports
of nourishment with a bit of bread,
a bourbon, a burrito bowl, a nipple,

a penis. I take in and in like oceans,
our landfills. My belly and arms swell,
striate like felled logs. Consider

the common inclination to love
into submission: "hush, baby."
I do this for myself when I masturbate

to fall asleep. I have been a woman
for some time now, a uterine cavern,
an acute sense of danger. I want

to be a mother unlike my own,
and I am ashamed to think I think
so little of her

resilience, her desperate love of me.
I do not want to bear a child,
because I do not want to feel

never alone. I'm so American I dream
of children discarded.
What happens to a child detained?

How many can I be a home to?

Portrait in the Lone Star

Sometimes two women meet and smile for no one else.

I looked into the open cleft of a lover and watched
the month's first rivulet descend as she called
on my tongue's continued praise.

In the world outside of plush duvets and soft bedfellows,
men with knives call tides of blood from daughters.

I don't know what I would do
if a man who looked like my daddy hated me,
hated my sex all the more because I did not want him
to have it, or because I have wanted a woman too—

wanted to roll a body out of, unclasp the straps.

What if the only time a black man loves me
is when I'm dressing his wounds?

Or, on a given day, I prefer the sweet humidity of a lipsticked breath,
the ice trail on a summer belly?

Somewhere near the home I left, two women lie together
openly in bayou humidity, croon in the lovers' spit.

Later, one's father unclasped the straps, rolled their bodies
out of a red Kia. Did she ever call him daddy?

Was it like the first time he held her?

Those bodies near the dumpster, faces facing or turned.
I like to believe the lovers' last acts were defiant, protective.
The women battered—him, a door to break through.

Self-Portrait as a Recurring Reflection Elongated like a Length of Vertebrae

after *A Man Ray Version of Man Ray* by Imogen Cunningham

It was easy to learn to drink. Find some privacy, keep a steady pace.
I was warned.
The cabinet told me no one would notice.

*

I taught myself to write a metaphor:
take something that gives you heat
and cast it in an observable body:

my lover is a spider

loosing silk into my palm.

*

It has taken me a long time to learn desire itself

is not monstrous,

but indulgence in ritual
without replenishment

is deadly.

My body swelled with spirits,
my teeth splintered
my gums blistered.

I've been practicing curses more than half my life.

Pour the bourbon. Light the match.
Roast the mouth.
Inhale, exhale, sip.

Blessings and curses are sisters—

*

There were times I could say no to myself.
Now my best-self whispers counsel.

*

I do keep trying
to save my life.

*

My girlhood was heather-colored,
a healing bruise.

I remember, now,
how much light I can create.

*

I never forget the beauty in viscera or the pickled parts of things.

*

The best thing I have ever learned to do is love
patiently. It is a kind of gardening,

coaxing joy from another human—
a kind of conjuring to appear
a blossom
of recognition in a beloved's face.

*

I didn't learn to love a partner by watching my parents.
I learned by remembering the lovers I sent away—
what I broke and tried to piece back together
while I was a drunk getting drunker.

*

More than once, I have been a barroom destroyer.

Now, I listen to my sweethearts' secrets, collect baubles
to offer, and say true hard things—
earnest things: your life is yours,
I'd like to walk with you a ways.

*

I would trade the ability to disassemble for the power to protect.
Blessed with this,

I could unlearn,
loose magic like spent seed,

douse the wreckage in rye.

II

For Dawn Wooten

I have the good fortune to be free:

to choose,

to have part of my cervix intact,

to change the locks after
I'm attacked.

Somebody offered me a karate class.

I could still, with a little more
of the luck I've already enjoyed,

say yes to a man—
to a little sugar.
Nobody has a life without a woman's blood.

I could still go under and come out whole
enough to make
another whole life—

a child to place to my mother's bosom—
Oh, to be free

enough to pick apart a rapist
man-in-charge, or

a god-doctor
with some script for all the reasons

he knows life is his enough to give
or take

like a kiss, or a breath.
Like a wave: to drown, uncover, or cover up.

An Abortion Ban

is a body snatcher,
is an ethnic cleansing.

The uterus is a cave,
is an incubator, is a vault,

is a self-destructing bomb,
is a thoroughfare.

Semen is an innocent bystander.
Penises are just boys being.

A woman is a vestibule.

A judge is a strict father,
is Joseph awed by his father's creation,

is Joseph relieved of fault,
is Joseph saving face.

A woman is a support beam.
A girl is a receptacle.

A fetus without lungs is an unlucky horseshoe.
A fetus in a homeless woman is an empty pillowcase.

An embryo is a fingernail.
A fetus is a jail.

A woman who miscarries is a quarterback—
executed. Point blank.

A woman with a felony is insulation.
An angry man with a staircase is a felony-maker.

A livebirth with a dead mother is a school lunch.
A stillbirth is a twenty-thousand-dollar bill.

A pregnant black woman is a dead black woman.
A black woman who miscarries is a dead crow.

A state legislature is a vulture.
A choice is a liability.

A Planned Parenthood is a desert.
A Planned Parenthood is an oasis.

A woman is a treasure chest.
A woman is a former voter.

A uterus is a leash.
A stillbirth is a tether.

A thirteen-year-old is a child. Only that.
A woman is a bloom.

A seed is an explosive.
Fertilizer is a shackle.

A woman is a target.
A uterus is a target.
A felon is a target.

Self-Portrait as an Atlas Moth at the Bar

The boys get mad: *Tease.*
I'm shameless.

I dance to sweat, rustle
every scale on my wings.

I use the moon to navigate
the night, follow flashes,

lit specks, neon for my flight.
I came to fill up

my lungs, fill up my blood,
fill up my head with night noise.

Anatomy of a Fish Hook

> *. . . how can I defend myself against what I want?*
> —Henri Cole

I fix my mouth to gather you
as our-other-selves stand in a doorway
eyeing us; inside—here—is a flurry of embers.
My touch amuses you—
down, up; hard, quiet. "I'm close," you whisper.
I palm your knee, stroke your throat,
and you remain whole as a mercy—
you are unequaled restraint—only the briefest flinch—
my lip slightly confused by the surfeit:
salt, water, muscle, saliva, fructose.

Ask yourself, are you sadder here outside
your alliances, weaning me from your thigh
(Clung on in a soulless coming), fear sprinkling
poison around you (Somebody near),
than when—with a king's ransom, a tongue,
paradise—you could hide your life, divide
it from a household peopled with closed mouths,
my barb fixed to your porous pink?

The Field of Blood

In the hospital, the man I love
lowers his eyes. Catheter. Cotton.
I join his mother for a walk.

If I were your mother,
I'd tell you not to marry him.
My own mother says

I can't stay with a sick man.
You want to fix everything.
Why should we leave good things broken?

*

On some night, my love says
I wouldn't want to be black. I—
I try to understand how he could

call blackness the burden,
not the whiteness heaped on top of it.
Blackness is not a failure

of the body. I bleed daily
for a month,
produce a liver-shaped thing.

He rinses his blood
with a chemical cocktail
every third Thursday.

We make nothing   no child
no pacts—but distance,
until we both lose.

*

On some day, in our home,
my love says our child
would not be black.

But we're American,
I think, and say
she would.

*

He thinks we understand each
other because of his illness
and my blackness,
but my blackness
does not make me sick.
Love has betrayed my heart.

*

I'm sure Judas loved Jesus, but fear is a tyrant.
In this story, you're Judas and I'm Judas too.

A cynic would say he just loved money more.
But what would they say to the field of blood?

I loved my man and our cats but the girl in my chest
will always chase the storm in the field, abandon

the ghost in the house, leave the blood and water
running in the bathtub and hair on the floor, walk

into the warm spring night in a blackout, follow the moon
down the sidewalk—eyes glinting like the backyard cougars

of my youth—and leave you with your bare heart
and your mended bones waiting for me

to come back. A version of me will leave and let the felines
starve because the beast in me does not want to be needed.

A cat's cry mimics an infant's cry.
I like to think I could deny even this.

Why I Meant It When I Said I Didn't Want Kids While You, Wanting Them and Me, Insisted I Did

I imagine spreading my bones, a baby,
then you at the birth going blind.

You pick up the baby and swing her around
in the park. You lose control of your hands:

she enters the air, and your bodies tumble.
You do your best to parachute beneath her.

I wonder what you think about our black baby
with your white mother. About your black woman

and her black child. I imagine
—because imagine is all I can do with the future—

you unable to drink, your atrophy,
and me wiping your face like an old man's wife.

I see myself in the park with our black baby
without you.

The Disappearing Field

After her husband dies, we drive
to the bird sanctuary to breathe

and walk awhile, to praise
the sparrows' their play.

Respite. We've just turned thirty
and death, which happens to everyone

else, has come. The shore
along the sanctuary

is empty. The waves turn over,
follow water, like years. *What next*?

Radiation arrived before cold storage,
so there will be no sibling

to the lost almost-child. A full-grown
sage thrasher flies by, a dappled

shell remnant clasped in her feathers.
We walk along the shore talking

chemo and inviable nests, not the flowers
for the funeral, but fibrous growths. Every

body is in disrepair. A gander limps
across the visible street. A gaggle waddles

in loose phalanx around a row of port-a-johns,
fills the disappearing field behind a stranger

as we wander. Our two bodies empty
of bodies. A friend and a widow on the shore.

To Deliver All Stillborn Safely

after *Sophie with Kittens* by Maude Schuyler Clay

I can't afford to have all my wisdom teeth extracted at once
but I need to have the rot removed.

When I consider pregnancy, I think of American rot,
not the babies but the people cop-murdered in the streets and
governments saving rapists' fruit to spite the women bearing it.

It stinks of God and Mary.

Don't you know He may enter
any vessel and raise flesh or fire?
Maybe it's passé to be angry with God,
but fury is part and parcel of love.

These governments would force the second coming—
as if God couldn't raise another son from clay.

Down the maternity halls black women are dying.

In my nightmare, twin black boys erupt from my pelvis
—through bone, flesh, and pubic hair—
form igneous rock when they hit the air.

This must be what I think of my unclean womanhood.

This uterus, a spout.
The pressure so great I can't completely close my mouth.

Lavender Menace Adopts a Black Boy

In summer black boy burns. Say,
black boy takes shelter. See his locked
hair fairy. See him. See him wash
his hands and brush his teeth.
See his smile shatter light.
Imagine summer camp. Black boy afloat
in Lake Michigan. Black boy
piñata. Black boys dance. Death drop.
A black boy is confetti. Black boy could be
a first cousin once removed.
Black boy would be ten now.
Or twelve. Black boy looks
like a father he's never seen. Black boy
is a grandma's boy. He is amalgam.
Black boy is dragonfly: brilliant, iridescent,
conspicuous in flight. 24,000
ommatidia. Black boy is anther
and filament. Black boy is a tyger,
tyger. Adopted black boy is a steal.
$17k. Black boy is waiting. Is chicken
chest. Black boy is grandfather-clock tall. Black
boy is never a clock tower. Black boy

is egret wings. Is flying. Is his father's
arms. Black boy is lisp and puppy scented.
Black boy is whipping boy.
Black boy is billy goat's gruff. Black boy's first
home is ragdoll, is a closet corner,
is tender purple. Black boy is plum pit,
walnut hull. Black boy is *curupira*.
Black boy is a dark city, is an open
window, is a roving squad car, is crashing
glass and song. A single black boy is the
softest avocado in the market.

Lavender Menace Considers the Lovers in the Photograph

after *Teddy and Chris* by Preston Gannaway

The men nestle, one inched in to the cleft of his love's thighs.
They wait under the eye of the sun, in the bull's eye
of the camera's lens, as a white witness documents black
love on a late spring day in Chesapeake, Virginia.

One, eyes closed, lips resting against his fellow's cheekbone.
The other eyes open stares forward soft-browed
as if he's just opened his eyes;
two moles make a bass clef of the curve of his left eye;

Open exposure in this one frame. Loose clothes betray
a slim collarbone, a meaty bicep, two modest black
bellies sun-coppered and hairy, the slightest catch
in a fold; a clasp on an elbow. The lovers, caught,

lean into each other away from the leaves
in front of the building, hold their spot
on the blacktop of the complex's parking lot.
Locked as if in bronze.

I have never seen a monument like this:
Durag and chinstrap mustache, brawn-armed
bear with a fresh, tight fade. I've lived at the corner
of Confederate and Lincoln, spat on the stone feet

of a gynecological barbarian, seen equestrians
erected high above men's heads, but never yet two
sleek wide noses or one man's neck tilted in supplication,
mouth slit open to let the air dart in, hands wound

lightly around a waist and lower back, knuckles alit
on a broad Dockered thigh, two men spun
like blossoming vines shining in the splendor
of two like soldiers in love. In light, not shadow.

But here the woman's eye has arrested
our fellows in dewy day, without labored sweat or defiant glances,
not off guard or posed but seeming free and seeming
safe in the baleen of each other's embrace.

III

American Girl Moves

I drive 900 daylight miles from Chicago
to Columbia, South Carolina, away
from my city rife with escape routes. South,

along the lake, past Kenwood, the Illiana Interchange,
through Ohio, through Kentucky. I think of Sandra Bland
who turned her blinker on or didn't—

who ended up alone in a cell, dead
with a pack of white men around her cage.
American girl drives a U-Haul across the country,

in which she is black before American,
black before woman. I bring a lover
who is white and black, who is City of Big Shoulders,

who is bold and lesbian and Jewish and American
and a princess. We American girls laugh,
listen for sirens,

sit susceptible to whiteness, blackness, and the men
in the motel rooms surrounding the one we share. Our
American girls huddle around cigarettes, retreat

from the man outside who assures *I'm not a cop.*
As if either way is a comfort. *Which room are you in?*
The Fort Jackson Days Inn, a prime spot for porn-making,

smells like thirty years of cigarette smoke. We are afraid
we might be hurt, like so many people:
spines torn, contorted into art pieces, massacred

in AME churches, flung like dolls
at pool parties, slung across classrooms, finger raped
by police officers, forced to fellate police officers.

Accused and accused and the news hangs on their skin.
American girl fears for her life. We girls—
targets on radar, small lights blinking: *I'm here, I'm here.*

[black]*

what do I know about being [   ]
but my mother's hand and mine

but my sister's back in her white white wedding dress
(her newly widowed face under new white hair)

but my brother's [   ] boy feet running running
against the NES power pad

(didn't know what was chasing him)
I knew it meant Dad

would visit and the boys would be boys
the finger's narrow escape from fire-

crackers mommy in the night with fire-
flies I caught

my [   ] meant country club
kids got out of the pool and I didn't notice until years later

but what do I know
may as well be white

except my grandmother washed white
women's floors and was common poor

except *shawty what yo name is?* and *you talk white, you stuck-up bitch*
but what do I know about [   ]

but my obese "african american" woman fibroids
or the policeman's gun to my face

the [   ] policewoman, saying
but what you really gon' be college girl?

or a white man who loves me and is
noticing my [   ]*ness a lot less lately*

or another [   ] woman trying to check me
on any given day in my grown-ass life

girl don't
you say: *oh, she's basically white*

and I know you're worried
we can't both exist

in some rooms, you know,
even the fact of the conversation is treason

*

[a shadow] [midnight with a new moon] [well bottom] [hottentot berry baker jackson] [coal] [2 million American prisoners] [Baldwin Lorde hooks Morrison]

"Praise the Lord for all dead things;

they cannot speak for themselves."

A woman speaks to her grandfathers in the photo:

What does your voice sound like?

Granddad:

Grandpa:

How old were you when you died?

Granddad:

Grandpa:

Did you ever say no to a white man?

Granddad:

Grandpa:

Did you ever hit your wife?

Granddad: . . .

Grandpa:

How many times?

Granddad:

Grandpa: . . .

Self-Portrait as an Octopus

In which every arm I have holds myself.
In which I dream
of rape and turn a deep mulberry.
In which one heart stops.
In which I take my mate's inseminating arm.
In which I begin to eat in preparation for survival.
In which I brood,
lay a small dense lump,
benign, engorged.

Port of Entry

St. Helena Island, SC, 1998

My mother took me to an island once.
I remember the thick, how dark
the forest can be, how canopy

the stars. My body like panties, then.
What web and stretchable.
What prevention.

I was just a visitor there.
My little room, that vessel, its arms
its hips,

their sucking
whirlpool surrounded
by ocean and hanging moss.

We searched for our faces among strangers;
we looked first through the church yard.
Tombstones will tell you where your hyoid split,

who taught your lips, your nose.
Are there more of my grandfather's people here?
Is this where our women wove earth into toys?

Do these trees know?
Do these trees know the grazing hem, the line
between sweet heat and deep sweat?

The woman('s) sex. Her hanging. They must.
Her hair is made of them.
Her hands, roots.

Mine is the hemline. But for the grace,
my dress may have lifted
as rope pulled at my neck.

My mother taught
me nothing about how to invite.
Only to add oil.

Girl Born with Cleft Palate Turns Ten, Divines for Water in Her Backyard

Y the shape of a discarded branch. Y over the dog dung spread in the yard's overgrowth. Y of two arms reaching out to slake their sweat in the sun. She cannot hear the voice of God, though her mother prays for her each morning. Sixteen dental surgeries and she has recovered perfect hearing, recalls the space after death. Y links the passage to the middle ear. She cannot hear the voice of God, though she knew it in her swaddling clothes. Whip-thin. Her now functional mechanisms: tongue, teeth, nose, uvula, the inner ear, gnash a prayer: "lead me to water, lead me to God" while she wanders her backyard with a divining rod.

Mockingbird

My mother lets me look through her jewelry boxes when I visit, tells me about the woman who sold her the Roman glass, about the resale shop where she found the switchblade, the turquoise ring she gave to my father and then to me. She bought me a piano for my thirteenth birthday, an upright. She framed a jazz man and put it up on the wall for me to see his black fingers on its black keys.

My mother laughs loudly, reveals her crowded teeth. She loves the giant mole on her lip and her haint grandma who she says kissed it there. Once I bucked at her, and she stared me down. My mother will cause a scene anywhere. She respects children and suspects adults. She puts God before all of man, including her children.

Once my mother fell down a flight of stairs. Once my mother was a president. Once my mother bought my debt. Once she came to me with a suitcase and a two-dollar fedora, her little arms like pussy willow branches in her leopard print coat. She tells me I should be happy; her mother called her all types of whore.

She's feast or famine. She does just what she wants. She is sunlight on wide white walls and amber oil and glass. She came to me with her suitcase and a smile reminding me she'd lost everything—even almost her sister, who talks to people no one else can see, even her son who didn't die, but wouldn't let her stay.

My mother, spitfire, African dancer, executive director. Once my mother passed out at work. Once she stopped taking her medication. Once she thought she had breast cancer. Once she needed money so we took in a boarder. She would have parties and I'd take shelter on the roof. Once my mother was my best friend. Once we didn't talk for a year. Once she gave me all the poems she ever wrote. Once my mom did a one-woman tour of her one-woman show across the state. Once she told me my home is where she is.

And in every bathroom of hers is an orange tin of Murray's hair dressing, short vials of Egyptian oils, a towel for a floor mat, rings and beaded necklaces, heavy amber and gold earrings, goat's milk soap, Dr. Bronner's peppermint soap, lavender soap, upended tin tops full of ash, cigarette butts in the toilet bowl, a swollen Bible on the bathtub, candles with ash and crisp wicks, some knick-knacky little black Jemima and a small black tchotchke, a picture of a smiling black girl, and a thin film cast by oil and hair and powder and lipsticks and pet hair and dander and living alone.

Sunday Morning

Hunger and the radio call us to the kitchenette.
Mama and that nasty-ass Bill at the table
with paring knife and lime sipping gin already.
Mama say, “Go ’head. Show Bill what all you can do.”

Mama and that nasty-ass Bill at the table
watch me drop my hip like little Sally Walker.
Mama say, “Go ’head, show Bill what all you can do.”
Twist and twirl. Blossoming at ten, I can tear.

Watch me drop my hip like little Sally Walker
with a paring knife and lime. Watch me
twist and twirl in time. Blossom, tear.
Hunger and the radio call us to the kitchenette.

Girl Secrets in Her Own Cocoon

To have a door! The back of which she could
wake to, smile at, brush her girl lips and hips
against. At night, she'd sit cross-legged
on the floor, press her knees to the door's face.
In her room, she'd deny her mother
entry, adorn herself in costume jewels
and pick her hair out round. She'd say yes
to her own face, neither too dark nor too much her
daddy's. In her mirror, she'd perfect her
smile—with teeth, without—smack her lips,
play woman without her mother's boyfriend
telling her *feed me a little a this*
fish. She'd take her cue from Martha Reeves,
jerk and gyrate. She wouldn't need *nowhere to run*.

Recovery

If it's recovery you want, go to the night. You are five or six. Go to the night and grab your mother before she hits the wall. Go through the wall and disappear your father's hands. *If you can't use them right, you can't have them till morning.* Put his paws in the hideaway where you keep your disappearance kit: flashlight, clean panties.

Or, *recover* as in to pull from wreckage. Go to the night you remember and pull the child from the bed. Over ice cream, tell her: *They're just a possibility, not a rule. None of this is a curse.* Then hand her a kazoo.

Or, *recover* as in *re-cover*. Bury the night, the yelp. The thump is a tennis ball or a Bible. Is a missing shoe or a man's head. Put on your helmet and go back to sleep. Bury it with your own undocumented trespasses, neither forgotten nor forgiven.

Caregiving

An old man is haunted by his living mother. She wanders her house outside or fully inside of her mind. A bleach-clean nightgown. Looking for lost money, her dead mother. Calling his name *what should I do?*

In her ninth decade, what's a mother to do but echo?

There's sweetness in rot. Like the oranges K— brought for Christmas: bright and hardening by January—wrinkled, shriveling, still moist inside. The breast and pure white brassiere. Her skin and diaper.

It's clean where her lost breasts have gone. Who will take care of this man who blushes to dress his mother?

I Take Myself for Walks

I wake up alone every morning.
I go to sleep alone every night.

I count sleeping pills.
I count every pill I can find

and conjure a friend who hanged himself.
I'm years older than he was when he died.

I don't want to kill myself.
I wake up alone and take myself

for walks. I listen to podcasts
and cry at well-told stories.

I take myself for walks hoping to help.
I take myself for walks and talk to God.

I talk to Him when I'm alone, alone
like when I'm walking down a hospital corridor.

I talk to Him when I come to a crossroads.
I talk to Him because I know my secrets will be safe.

He doesn't talk back. He doesn't have to
exist to exist.

What good is a god you can't trust?
I can make his lack of intervention

a scapegoat, and I can make my boons his glory.
We're all just telling stories.

Dear Father,

the stories I told myself about you as a girl have kept me soft-hearted for my
own father despite his sins, despite his failures. We talk often, so I can talk
to you from time to time. I can, like all your children, absolve you when you
abandon one of your kids or beat a woman sworn by love and law to keep you.
Or when your absence is the rule and my praise is still expected. I do know that
if I broke down here just outside of Blacksburg my father would bring himself
here—or show by proxy. A man I can trust. And you—no matter what story
I told my mother, would get the glory. Because the story is we are all you by
proxy. We are, like all roads, both a thing all our own and a thing in between.

The Big Water

I want to say yes to the sea and live
with the knowledge that I am small.

I live with my knowledge, small despite
my good learning. The truth is hard.

With all my costly living, truth is still hard.
Sober, I find my mind in disarray.

To save my life, I undress this disarray.
Fear babbles beneath. Terror cannot protect.

Terror cannot protect like anger does,
and a vulnerable life leaves room for love.

A vulnerable life leaves room for you
to love yourself enough to lose someone.

To love yourself enough to lose someone is
to become the open sea, not the estuary.

ACKNOWLEDGMENTS

Thank you to the editors and publications that published these poems, sometimes with different titles and in earlier forms.

Blackbird: "Baptism"

Boston Review: "An Abortion Ban" and "The Field of Blood"

Blood Orange Review: "Lavender Menace Adopts a Black Boy," "Lavender Menace Considers Adoption in the Trump Era," and "Daddy on the Sofa"

Foglifter: "Mockingbird"

Home Is Where You Queer Your Heart, Foglifter Press: "Lavender Menace Considers the Lovers in the Photograph" (originally "The Lovers in the Photograph")

Jet Fuel Review: "Portrait in the Lone Star"

Kettle Blue Review: "American Girl Moves" and "The Disappearing Field" (originally "Montrose Beach, Before the Funeral")

Muzzle Magazine; republished in *Best New Poets, 2019* (University of Virginia Press): "[black]*" (originally "[midnight with a new moon]")

Potomac Review: "Musing on Lilith Lost to Time"

Quiet Lunch: "Sunday Morning" (originally "WKRB Brooklyn, Sunday Morning")

South Carolina Review: "Praise the Lord for all dead things" and "Girl Born with Cleft Palate Turns Ten, Divines for Water in Her Backyard"

Poem-a-Day at Poets.org: "Why Don't You Parent a Little?"

ReDivider: "The Big Water" and "Long Live the Queen" (originally "Nest")
RHINO: "Girl Secrets in Her Own Cocoon" and "Eviction"

GRATITUDE

Thank you, dear reader, for your dime, your time, and your attention. Thank you for bringing your head and heart here.

Thank you to my parents for your encouragement, your honesty, for working as hard as you do, and for your relentless love. To my chosen family: to Rachel for a lifetime; to Heather for growing up with me.

To my Chicago poetry community: Aricka Foreman, Kenyatta Rogers, and Keith S. Wilson. Thanks to Vox Ferus, particularly Marty McConnell and Erica Dreisbach.

To the RHINO community, including Ralph Hamilton, for continuing to ask for my book; to Angela Narciso Torres, for your keen editorial eye. Thank you, Jacob Saenz, for the walks and talks, for your gingerly placed questions, and for insisting on the knife.

To Cave Canem: Toi Derricote and Cornelius Eady, thank you for making a home for us. To Laura Swearingen-Steadwell, Kateema Lee, Casey Rocheteau, Natasha Ria El-Scari, Makalani Bandele, Sasha Warner Barry, Amber Flora Thomas, Robin Coste Lewis, Evie Shockley, Chris Abani, Dante Micheaux, Patricia Smith, and Nate Marshall.

The Watering Hole Tribe, especially Jericho Brown, Nicole Homer, Candice Wiley, Monifa Lemons, Jennifer Bartell Boykin, and Teri Elam.

The University of South Carolina MFA cohorts 2015–2018, especially Lauren Rose Clark and Catherine Ntube. To the USC MFA faculty, especially Sam Amadon and Nikky Finney.

Thank you to Callaloo, Vermont Studio Center, and the MacDowell Colony. Thank you to the Institute for African American Research at the University of South Carolina and to the Community of Writers. Thank you to everyone who offered me space to think and write.

Thank you to Haymarket Books.

NOTES

"Baptism": This poem references the song "Don"t Smoke in Bed," performed by Nina Simone on *Little Girl Blue.*

"For Dawn Wooten": In an official complaint, Wooten stated that the International Child Development Centre was performing hysterectomies on people without their informed consent, referring to the doctor who allegedly performed them, a Georgia gynecologist, Dr. Mahendra Amin, as the "uterus collector." For more, see Erin Corbett, "New Details Have Emerged about the ICE Whistleblower Who Witnessed Mass Hysterectomies," Refinery29.com, September 17, 2020.

"Port of Entry": The hyoid is the U-shaped bone of the neck that is fractured in one-third of all homicides by strangulation. On this basis, postmortem detection of hyoid fracture is relevant to the diagnosis of strangulation. It is often used to identify whether a person was hanged. For more, see M. S. Pollanen and D. A. Chiasson, "Fracture of the Hyoid Bone in Strangulation," *Journal of Forensic Science* 41, no. 1 (January 1996): 110–13.

"Portrait in the Lone Star": James Cosby, age forty-six, bludgeoned his daughter Britney Cosby to death and shot her lover, Crystal Jackson, on March 6, before dumping the bodies near the ferry gate in Port Bolivar, Texas, police believe. See Sasha Goldstein, "Texas Dad Killed Daughter, Her Lesbian Lover because He Disliked That She Was Gay," *New York Daily News*, March 14, 2014.

"American Girl Moves" includes references to various acts of violence incurred by black people from 2014 to present. For more information, look to links or just listen to the news. See, for instance, David Collins, "Neurosurgeon: Freddie Grey Suffered Complete Spinal Cord Injury," WBALTV.com, December 11, 2015. Kenneth Goldsmith used Michael Brown's autopsy as "poetry"; see Jillian Steinhauer, "Kenneth Goldsmith Remixes Michael Brown Autopsy Report as Poetry," Hyperallergic.com, March 16, 2015. Reference to the shooting at Mother Emanuel, see Matt Ford and Adam Chandler, "'Hate Crime': A Mass Killing at a Historic Church," *Atlantic*, June 19, 2015. Reference to the beating of a student by an officer, see Aldref Ng, "Spring Valley School Officer Caught on Video Slamming South Carolina Student to Ground During Arrest; Officer Pulled from School," *New York Daily News*, October 27, 2015. Reference to officers raping people in police custody, see Eliott C. McLaughlin, Sara Sidner, and Michael Martinez, "Oklahoma City Cop Convicted of Rape Sentenced to 263 Years in Prison," CNN.com, January 22, 2016. Reference to police officers sexually abusing woman in custody, see Carlos Miller, "Nebraska Deputy Who Forced Woman to Perform Oral Sex," PINAC News, April 18, 2015.

"Praise the Lord for All Dead Things;: I believe the line "Praise the Lord for all dead things; they cannot speak for themselves," comes from Forrest Gander's *Deeds of Utmost Kindness.*

ABOUT THE AUTHOR

Maya Marshall is cofounder of *underbelly,* the journal on the practical magic of poetic revision. Marshall has served as artist in residence at Northwestern University and as faculty for the Loyola University Chicago creative writing program. She holds fellowships from MacDowell, Vermont Studio Center, Callaloo, the Watering Hole, Community of Writers, and Cave Canem. She is the author of the chapbook *Secondhand* (Dancing Girl Press, 2016). Her writing appears in *Best New Poets 2019, Blood Orange Review, ReDivider, Muzzle Magazine, RHINO, Potomac Review, Blackbird,* and elsewhere. She teaches at Emory University.

ABOUT HAYMARKET BOOKS

Haymarket Books is a radical, independent, nonprofit book publisher based in Chicago. Our mission is to publish books that contribute to struggles for social and economic justice. We strive to make our books a vibrant and organic part of social movements and the education and development of a critical, engaged, international left.

We take inspiration and courage from our namesakes, the Haymarket martyrs, who gave their lives fighting for a better world. Their 1886 struggle for the eight-hour day—which gave us May Day, the international workers' holiday—reminds workers around the world that ordinary people can organize and struggle for their own liberation. These struggles continue today across the globe—struggles against oppression, exploitation, poverty, and war.

Since our founding in 2001, Haymarket Books has published more than five hundred titles. Radically independent, we seek to drive a wedge into the risk-averse world of corporate book publishing. Our authors include Noam Chomsky, Arundhati Roy, Rebecca Solnit, Angela Y. Davis, Howard Zinn, Amy Goodman, Wallace Shawn, Mike Davis, Winona LaDuke, Ilan Pappé, Richard Wolff, Dave Zirin, Keeanga-Yamahtta Taylor, Nick Turse, Dahr Jamail, David Barsamian, Elizabeth Laird, Amira Hass, Mark Steel, Avi Lewis, Naomi Klein, and Neil Davidson. We are also the trade publishers of the acclaimed Historical Materialism Book Series and of Dispatch Books.

ALSO AVAILABLE FROM HAYMARKET BOOKS

The Billboard by Natalie Y. Moore, foreword by Imani Perry

The Body Family by Hope Wabuke

Build Yourself a Boat by Camonghne Felix

DEAR GOD. DEAR BONES. DEAR YELLOW. by Noor Hindi

Doppelgangbanger by Cortney Lamar Charleston

Electric Arches by Eve L. Ewing

Mama Phife Represents: A Memoir by Cheryl Boyce-Taylor

So We Can Know: Writers of Color on Pregnancy, Loss, Abortion, and Birth edited by aracelis girmay

Too Much Midnight by Krista Franklin

Undivided Rights: Women of Color Organizing for Reproductive Justice by Marlene Gerber Fried, Elena Gutiérrez, Loretta Ross, and Jael Silliman